06.17

This book should be returned/renewed by the
latest date shown above. Overdue items incur
charges which prevent self-service renewals.
Please contact the library.

Wandsworth Libraries
24 hour Renewal Hotline
01159 293388
www.wandsworth.gov.uk

PRIMERS:
Volume Two

PRIMERS:
Volume Two

Ben Bransfield
Cynthia Miller
Marvin Thompson

Selected by Jacob Sam-La Rose
and Jane Commane

Nine
Arches
Press

Primers: Volume Two

Ben Bransfield, Cynthia Miller and Marvin Thompson

Edited by Jacob Sam-La Rose and Jane Commane

ISBN: 978-1-911027-18-8

Cover artwork / Primers logo © 3Men²
www.3men.co.uk

First published April 2017 by:

Nine Arches Press
PO Box 6269
Rugby
CV21 9NL
United Kingdom

www.ninearchespres

Printed in Britain by:
Imprint Digital

Nine Arches Press is supported using public funding by the National Lottery through Arts Council England.

Supported using public funding by
**ARTS COUNCIL
ENGLAND**

Primers: Volume Two

is produced in partnership with:

About the Selecting Editors:

Jacob Sam-La Rose was born in London in 1976. He was managing director of a web development studio before becoming a freelance writer and editor. He is the Artistic Director of the London Teenage Poetry SLAM, Editor-in-Chief of Metaroar.com, and an editor for flipped eye press. He also facilitates a range of literature-in-education, creative writing and spoken word programmes through schools, arts centres and other institutions. His work has appeared in many anthologies and journals, including *Identity Parade: New British & Irish Poets* (Bloodaxe), *Poems For Love* (Penguin), *I Have Found a Song* (Enitharmon Press), *Red* (Peepal Tree), *Learn Then Burn: The Ultimate Poetry Guide for the High School or College Classroom* (Write Bloody) and Michael Rosen's *A-Z: The Best Children's Poetry from Agard to Zephaniah* (Puffin). His pamphlet *Communion* was a Poetry Book Society Pamphlet Choice in 2006. *Breaking Silence* (Bloodaxe Books, 2011), his first book-length collection, was shortlisted for both the Forward Prize for Best First Collection and the Fenton Aldeburgh First Collection Prize 2012.

Jane Commane was born in Coventry and lives and works in Warwickshire. Her poems have been published in *Tears in the Fence, And Other Poems, Iota, Anon, The Stare's Nest* and the *Morning Star* and collected in *Best British Poetry 2011* and *Lung Jazz: Young British Poets for Oxfam*. Jane is editor at Nine Arches Press and co-editor of *Under the Radar* magazine.

CONTENTS

Marvin Thompson

FOREWORD

Consider the *Primers* countdown: three selected poets, a second book published, one copy in your hand. We – Nine Arches Press, the Poetry School and selecting editor Jacob Sam-La Rose – are delighted to launch the second volume in our Primers mentoring and publishing series, and welcome you to our selected poets' worlds.

This most recent *Primers* scheme brought in a rich and appealing menu of new poetry for us to consider and ponder over during the autumn and winter of 2016. Our first round of selections produced an initial long-longlist of just under a hundred promising submissions that we finessed into a longlist of just 28 poets. Our further reading and intense, enjoyable discussions resulted in the shortlist of ten, which included auspicious and thought-provoking new poetry from Emma Jeremy, Marjorie Lofti-Gill , Matthew Dixon, Michelle Penn, Miranda Peake, Paul Adrian, and Samuel Prince as well as our three finalists, Ben Bransfield, Cynthia Miller and Marvin Thompson.

What are the advantages, then, of a scheme like *Primers?* For one, the submissions process itself offers each poet who submits an assessment of their work, however brief that may be – whether it's simply 'No, not this time' or an encouraging 'Maybe, let's put this on the longlist' or perhaps even a resounding consensus of 'Oh yes, this MUST go on the shortlist!' from the selecting editors. Each decision has a value in evaluating original work at an important stage of its development. If you submitted poems to *Primers* and were not successful this year, you still took a giant step in doing something practical and positive to get your poems out there and under our collective consideration. Admiration is due to every single poet who took the time to refine and polish-up their six best poems and submit them to *Primers: Volume Two* – even if you didn't make any of the lists, you had the courage and confidence to put your work before us, and allow us the privilege of considering your poems. Well done. Keep going. These seemingly small steps matter, and are a most vital part of developing as a poet and writer.

Following our consideration of the initial submissions, we next embarked on the challenge of whittling a very talented shortlist of ten poets down to our final choices of just three. This process is pleasingly unpredictable; until we delve into a month of close reading, we don't know what the full submission of twenty poems from each poet will bring, or where this wider selection of poems will take us. It often feels like a voyage into new territories of poetry – and a rare chance to take a peek over the shoulders of a handful of talented poets to see what they've been working away on in their notebooks. *Primers* is certainly an opportunity to take the temperature of the wider poetry-writing ecosystem, and it seems safe to conclude from *Primers: Volume Two* that poetry is in rude health at this present time.

As we read and make choices, themes, ideas and common threads will abound; for every poet finding new and remarkable ways of making the personal universal, there will be others finding memorable and powerful ways to make the universal more personal. We are conscious too that *Primers* offers a unique opportunity to present together three distinct voices to a new readership, so a part of our consideration is also about curation; how our chosen three poets will work together, why each has something unique to offer the reader, and what dynamic will result from the combination of their work in one new volume. We certainly felt strongly when making those final decisions that the poems here by Ben, Cynthia, and Marvin will bring something equally irresistible and unrivalled to the table for the three-course poetry feast that is *Primers: Volume Two*.

As reader, you'll establish your own relationship with the work selected for this anthology. Ben drew us in with a poetry that is intimately entangled with place; poems that offer up tangible slices of lives lived, a celebration of family ties and personal portraits with all of their emotional complexities, but also sharp, unexpected turns. In Cynthia, we found a poet with a wide, expansive eye capable of attending to fine detail, very much alive to some of the most pertinent issues that fly close to the surface of our present-day experience (migration, personhood, cultural identity...) without being defined or bound by them. Marvin's engagement and experimentation with narrative and formal sequences immediately piqued our interest, while his characters and everything they allow him to interrogate captured us entirely. Marvin's Olivier Welsh is a mask within a mask; his alter ego, Tommy Mann, rises and falls under a spotlight focused boldly on race. Each has much to offer, and we look forward to the future of their work beyond these pages.

Congratulations to Ben, Cynthia and Marvin and may your launch be spectacular. Readers and fellow poets – we hope you enjoy the trip.

Julia Bird, The Poetry School
Jane Commane, Nine Arches Press
Jacob Sam-La Rose, Primers Selecting Editor

For further information about *Primers* and future opportunities as part of this publishing and mentoring scheme organised by The Poetry School with Nine Arches Press, please see: **www.poetryschool.com**

Ben Bransfield

Ben Bransfield was born in Shropshire in 1987 and now lives in London, where he works as a teacher. He read English at Brasenose College, Oxford, and received an MA from the Shakespeare Institute. His poems have appeared in publications including *The North, Obsessed with Pipework, Ash,* and have been placed in the Wenlock and Peterloo competitions. He was named a Teacher Trailblazer by the Poetry Society in 2015.

Greenhouse

Tomato gas blast: panels green and spidering
to beetle ticks, the pang and clack of fly on glass.

Within, the tepid brew of a scum-crusted tank,
frogspawn-clotted, lidless; terracotta pots brawl.

Without, that upturned bath against its side,
Granddad's greenhouse: best place to hide.

Granddad

How close to the setts did he hide?
Our sentry of the underdog, our national trust,
and his waddling warriors we knew from Farthing Wood
who could have a good go at a trapper's face.

I draw him out: there, in his camouflaged tent
on the third dark, fighting off the nodding off,
and thinking of me, perhaps, not yet born,
alert at the cut of an engine, a distant bark.

Palaeontology

A clay pipe in three parts:
outside the bone bleached bowl
not a trace of tobacco
and barely a seam on the straw.

Summon Southorn's girls crafting ribs
from the pug mill, Churchwardens
packed into saggars for days in the kiln,
for the Empire and those down the bank.

Uncle Graham *having a Broseley*,
the smoke of our gods, viced
and hanging from the left
but always lit from the right.

Churchwardens – tobacco pipes with long stems
saggars – boxes to protect ware being fired in a kiln

Broseley

In the distance: Buildwas Power Station;
the Iron Bridge, a napkin-ring over the Severn;
the beacon, pinned to the top of the Wrekin.
Eustace Rogers builds a coracle,
a tortoise shell or a Spartan shield;
Auntie Kay's boxer chases a hedgehog.
I can't see Legge's Hill or the jitty that runs down
to the donkeys, but there are Pat and Pat
putting pansies outside the front of the shop.
Down the road, the school buses are coming
back from Willy Brookes, the Ab Dab,
and through the window, just beyond the net,
Granddad tying his last wish to the banister,
Nan still halfway up the crescent with the shopping.

Garden Twine

They found it down the back
of the tumble dryer –

Auntie Jan, or the police,
during the inquest, or after.

I never saw its three ties –
bowline, clove hitch, slip –

a prayer for each of us grandkids.
This rosary hurt the most:

you'd left us no note, Granddad,
had been practising for weeks.

Paradise

If you took the bend too hard you'd miss it.
In the steeps of Coalbrookdale, one terrace row
nestled above those deeper furnaces, iron's home.
Your Hephaestus, *the Great Lady*, never moving
from her throne, her pocket bible just in reach
and pressing petals, the faded paisley armchair throw
behind her puckering neck and Clive,
her eldest, your uncle, straining leaves for tea.
The tale of Granddad climbing all the way up there
with ice cream wrapped in paper for you all.
The fossil, propping the garden gate open,
the megalithic stoned-in snail that was a dream
to helter-skelter with my doubter's finger,
wasn't nearly worth as much back then.

Glossary

Some years after your father had died
you were at the tiles around our gas fire

with linseed oil. Late morning,
The Supremes on the radio back in the kitchen

as your slow work with the cloth
brought up shine we'd never seen.

The fireplace now a sepulchre,
a gloss of pine and the petrol of beehives.

You could almost see your face in those tiles,
singe your lungs, let your hair go up.

SupaSnaps

The lady always called you *Ducky*
as you handed over our best moments
capped in pots no grander than cotton reels.
You never asked for matte, went five by seven
for special occasions, holidays at Clarach Bay.

Days later, in green or yellow envelopes
the size of posh purses, our lives in colour cut-out:
a deck unshuffled, and your quick flick through
the first few for a fingertip or a red eye
before we got home for a proper look.

You taught us to hold by the edge,
to leave no smudge. We never touched
the pouch of negatives, those genesis proofs
where we were X-ray, on fire, screaming
through the kitchen light.

Shaving with my Father

                        in the kitchen,
the sink without the bowl and only filled
like this for peeling spuds or soaking pans.
Velcro parting slowly, then a sparrow's bath
and the blade comes up clean, glides again.
Two bare chests, the mirror's snow-mowing,
stretching lip on gum to get the chin just right,
the run of neck now taut to stop the nicks.
Me, gently lifting out your white foam clots
to lather up my own face at your hip,
never minding all those auburn filings.
Your stinging *Denim* aftershave stopped burns.
The tissue's bond was blood. A clearing shared.
The fork's edge on my face still keeping time.

Amanita phalloides

Though I cannot bear a child of my own,
I might one day have a Death Cap mushroom.
White, with faint yellowish flesh below the cap,
he'll start out in mixed deciduous woodlands, under oak.

I know all parents think this of their own
but mine will be *the* fungi, with magical properties.
If, after check-ups of his hair-like hyphae,
mycologists concur that he's a spore-dropper –

not a shooter – I'll be fine with that.
If told he's only *reproductive parts,*
a fruit, or trolled with *bell-end toadstool, mulch,*
I'll drop my work and make us both a brew.

I'll give him space to grow his crowd of gills
though – despite the rational stats
that somewhere in the region of three thousand
larger fungi are to be found in the British Isles –

I'll still get nervous every summer's end,
when the druids and foragers might creep.
At times like these I fear I'll do as any parent might:
despite the fact that no known antidote exists –

that death can take twelve days
as cells of liver and kidney turn to mush –
I'll save my child their ceremonial knives,
their type specimen bags. I'll prove a father's love.

Delivery

Last night I dreamed I pushed you out of me.
It did not seem so strange. You weren't stillborn
this time, there was no cord about your neck,
no stoppered scream. There were no genes in you
but mine, and so, because it was a simple cure –
to halt the self-destruct that would be free
in you too soon, before you came of age –
they made me put out eyes that I had grown
from seed, then watch our red penance break
like waters from my knackered hairy knees.
I woke then peed a spurt in starts, where you
had been, where I had turned into that tree,
and wept to know you could not, would not, be.

Pac-a-mac

You were a body bag, shrink-wrapped.
I couldn't stand your toothless clasp,
the way those plastic sweating sleeves
sucked, clinging to marble skin,
throwing off the rain.

In bus shelters and verandas
I'd peel you off, like being born –
my waterproof, my navy caul –
prise limpet sweets from crusty pockets,
appalled at how you'd deflate.

You knew crunched-up crisp packets
from the pit of my satchel, were ready
to serve should clouds split open.
It's here now still: your stink, your itch,
elastic wrists, your damp shackle lips.

And to this day

there's a well down those woods
that feeds off tales of *stay aways*.

By nine our heads were knitted with them:
fireside legends, the edges of seats.

Chewing our nails, twisting our hair,
we'd conker scout the outer trees

but soon slip deeper
to a cooler place, that well of stone.

A check over the shoulders then
leaning in, up to no good with echoes,

things we'd longed to say all day.
Once spent of shout, we'd itch to do.

The once we did. *Pull up the bucket.*
See who could hoist it full and quickest.

The straining rope, riddled with rot,
coiling onto our pumps, until, at last,

its weeping pail hauled over with a groan.
Us flat out on our backs, about to laugh,

but for the bit of finger there inside.
That lock of hair. The miles from home.

Bedlington Terrier

After an iPhone photo taken in the Crooked Billet, Wimbledon

Let us assume a sheep was not involved,
that no dire wolf was up our grandam's pit.
What red terror had you painted down
the throat of those Northumbrian mines,
after rats? We have wept for your topknot,
whey-faced but clear of curd and cheesecloth.
We will not flock for a bite of your bark,
be told what you have lost, given a lead.
You are the last thing that we need right now.
Save us your purse of Bedlam wisdom,
lead us not into your Norman Cornish pasture
where, even now, one more coal-pup
lightens to liver, leaps. Just know your strength,
Lamb of God. You could kill your weight in dog.

Norman Cornish – Miner and artist, Spennymoor, Co. Durham (1919-2014)

Copper Calf

Full-tilt on the steep field
you feed on greens
as fully as your brothers do

but wander further
than the rest, to weigh
the balance of a branch

between your cattle lips
the way a dog might,
the way a large bird could.

What ground you have covered
copper calf, what market
you have pillaged

from pheasant and hare
to build your bulk.
Your ears twitch,

conduct their orchestra
of chomp and tear,
your several stomachs

even now at work
under your golden healing
fleece, your prize hide.

Your tail is a dancebrush,
scribing cooler air
with your short yarn

of half-baked flies and shit
that pours a thin stream
from your back-end tap.

Your mother watches me move
the way a mother might,
in a park, on a beach.

I could watch you for days,
learn to do with head and neck
the moves that are your trade.

Copper calf, what is a nettle to you,
a dandelion exploding
through a feast of grass?

I could smell the burnt sugar
of your skin through such fine felt,
could let your tongue melt on mine.

Cynthia Miller

Cynthia Miller is a Malaysian-American poet and brand strategist living in Birmingham. She has been shortlisted for the Bridport Prize, and her poetry has appeared in *Under the Radar* and The Emma Press *Anthology of Love*. When not writing poetry, she loves organising creative events that bring poetry to wider audiences in the city. As Co-Director of Verve, Birmingham's inaugural poetry and spoken word festival, she brings the festival to life through lively branding and marketing. She is also currently part of Room 204, Writing West Midlands' creative development programme for emerging writers.

Leave

Home is a weapon that you lift
to your shoulder, a cool promise
against your skin. Home is a
series of possibilities.

There are eviction notices in
graffiti: *get out*. There is a brick
through the window, there is
a man in every room in your house.

You'll be okay from here.
It's not a question.
You walk around in such thin skin
under a sky blue and headstrong.

There are paper tigers pacing the rafters.
You fear the front yard has turned
to quicksand. Someone's been planting
little bombs under the magnolia tree.

All your limbs are so heavy,
you have been running for days.
You have carried everyone you love,
and for so long, and over such distances.

Home is the wrongness of a muzzle
at the door, the heart's dark chamber,
it's climbing into the black mouth
of a lion and trusting him not to snap.

Yellow

After Ocean Vuong

"I brought my whole self to you. I am your mother."
– Maya Angelou, *Mom & Me & Mom*

1.

黃 means yellow, means honey dragonfruit,
    custard apple, salted durian, a wet star cut true.
And your name became my name: untameable forsythia,
    a ribbon twining between us. Let's play a name game
of cat's cradle from Wee to Ooi and Uy and Ng.
    Blame the British and Dutch clerks sweating
through their regulation shirts in some upriver Borneo outpost,
    whose ears couldn't tell the difference.

2.

Your skin
the leather of papaya

left too long on the branch,
single persimmon bulb.

Let's call you halogen fruit
that burned brightest.

Let's call you the girl
that made it out of there.

3.

Who needs jewels when you have
yellow that is ancient and imperial
that is banana cream paint
that is the end of a purpling bruise
that is the centre of the world
that is oo ooh I am
up to my neck in yellow
that is joy, sure –

4.

A square of sunflowers
soaked in sugar syrup,
the perfect colonial style house
we ached for, one beautiful
as a chiffon cake with
PTA mothers with perfect hair
who made sandwiches filled
with grape jam not beansprouts,
not growing French beans
in recycled milk gallons
by a chain link fence, not
sunning bedsheets in the yard –
what stupid sick roil of shame.
Yellow that is joy, sure, but history too.
Courage first.

5.

Whatever you do, don't burn out, she says in the garden
under the yellow rambutan tree, where we eat
mother of pearl sweetness by the prickly handful.
Moving is mourning. We are only together a short while,
she remarks, just travellers on the same path.
My mother is sulphur fruit, sharp and bright
as lightning in a dry season, a whole wildfire blowing hard
     out ahead,
clearing the way. Next to her, we are small hot stars
wheeling around fixed points. Sayang, love scorches
clean through you. May it never go out.
May you warm your body by it. May it be furious and shining,
backfire to any blaze barreling your way,
only a hot ache left in its place.

Drokpa

"Longing, we say, because desire is full / of endless distances."
– Robert Hass, 'Meditation at Lagunitas'

In another life, my father
must have been a nomad.
He drinks butter tea,
knows his way around a saddle,
turns the living room into open rangeland.
There are horses at the door,
nudging their big noses into the hallway,
familiar to him as brothers.
Everywhere we turn they are
stamping down the carpet, swinging wide,
sweating hard, and right in the centre
of that heaving bunch of muscle,
dad pours out the door like wind,
loose bridle, easy seat,
running like hell.
In Tibetan, *drokpa* means 'people of the solitudes',
as if solitude was open country.
In which we learn early
to lean into the gale, to forage old ground.
He does not dwell long,
disappears for seasons at a time
and we came to realise the way he loves
is the way a horse makes a break for it,
steaming, impatient, expectant,
body corded tight. Horses like clouds
scudding across fields of grass, wild iris,
lashed canvas. He takes off, bad back and all.
His heart opens like a valley.

Lupins

It never occurred to me
to ask where purple honey

               comes from but it must
               be the lupins that stand

like tiny sentries
at parade attention,

               sticks of blue raspberry
               rock candy, azalea jazz,

early plums, stars jangling
like spurs or new pennies,

               grape soda, lapis prayer, pokeberry
               plaits, soft and woollen,

salt spray of violet so heady
it hurts to look straight at it.

               Such indigo light
               like windfall fruit

rioting up the hill
and down to the sea.

               Some days
               their purple spines

are the only things
holding me up.

Cassandra

"How does it feel to be a problem?"
– Safiya Sinclair, 'Notes on the State of Virginia, III'

Open your news ticker mouth. Follow the prompter.
Books are full of men telling boys they're special;
    you are told *you know you want this.*

Remember how good it feels to burn.

The neighbours shifting their weight in the night
like horses and the fireman's bellow
                        a shiver through the folding house,
            collapsed lung, last breath rung like a bell
on the last rung of the ladder that would have held you, precious
    as a well in the desert.

All the men who love you and demand to hear it back,
        palms outstretched like the saints.
           You place careful words
between their lips like alms.

    Believe you me,
to care for yourself is also love.
See to your own oxygen mask first
before wondering what all of this burning does
to the heart and lungs of an animal. The pluck.

It's not the city on fire, it's you:
nothing left in this last brilliant blaze as planes
peel into the night off hot tarmac
and the boy you asked to the Sadie Hawkins dance
kisses you hard in the backseat of a borrowed car,

cottonmouth man coming through tall grass,
your whole body a match for his sandpaper kiss,
his square hand on your mouth. That's the night you realise
ecstasy looks a lot like disbelief.

The house alive on the hill. The deer jackknifing into trees.
        The flashlights bobbing
crisscross applesauce up the drive.

Say what you want.
Say what you know to be true.
        Better to unpetal a daisy
(he loves me, he loves me not).
                The horse is shot, or it is not.
                The gods listen, or they do not.
                The soldier returns home, or he does not.

                                Longing blooms, gangrenous.

So ask again in that wine dark,
                that sodium half-light.
    What is to become of us, Magic 8 girl?   Do we go on like this?
Swear it.
Yes. It is certain. It is decidedly so.

October Song

Tell me how good I look,
kiss each night with a bonfire
mouth. I slip into an equinox
dress, pear palette of ochre,

mustard sweetness, smoke, apples
full throated as birds in the trees.
Let the sun do its work,

rooting us home. I smooth
a hand over the dresses
hanging in my mother's closet,
mink and mauve and tea rose.

She is still in the north facing garden,
squatting over asters and saying,
all things need a little warmth.
Light up, old girl, light up.

The Impossible Physiology of the Free Diver

By the time this poem ends, the hummingbird
　　you're thinking of might be dead,
　　a hard-boiled ruby sweet in the bush.

　　　　　*

A billion heartbeats in a lifetime
is all we get; the slower your pulse
　　the longer you live.
Did you know the left lung shares
　　space with the heart, that
a free diver's lungs compresses
　　to the size of two apples?

　　　　　*

At Nicole's tenth birthday party,
　　among bright bathing suits,
　　pink lemonade blooming
where it spilled in the shallow end,
　　the sun a hot stone fruit,
　　I crossed my legs and sank
　　down in the community pool
to see how long I could hold my breath,
　　stop time, and just for a moment
　　I was a little god on the floor
　　of the world looking up.

　　　　　*

There is a flyer trapped
in the screen door that reassures:
You have so much more living to do.
A moment, please,
for the heart yammering away,
the heart standing on the porch,
the heart measuring breaths like levelling sugar
for a batter, the heart saying
why don't you come in from the cold.
And how later a mother wakes
in the night to her two year old's cough,
carrying him in her arms
to the steamed-up bathroom,
scrabbling for Vicks,
panic as big as the sea, its inevitable gravity,
poor lungs the size of a crabapple,
her hummingbird heart in her mouth.
She rucks up his shirt, touches his small back.
How the heart murmurs
breathe, baby, breathe.

How to Run Away

after Zeina Hashem Beck

Disappear –
I dreamt of Amelia Earhart again,
slipping in the night
under the full lip of the sea.

Gospel Oak –
Imagine a choir of trees
peeling their arms away in song,
the train a groaning organ.

July –
We spend all summer digging up roots:
cicadas caught
in crisp amber.

Berries –
Like rain plink plinking
in a metal pail, the promise
of something sweet, preserved.

Clairvoyance –
The weekly horoscope:
quicksilver moon in Cancer,
the old tug of tides at my heart.

Naming –
A leaving litany of streets passed:
Alice Deal, Brandywine
Fessenden, Grafton, Gramercy.

Moving –
Rooting for a milk pan you swore
up and down we packed, familiar jiggle
of your arms, your tapioca skin.

Healing –
Find a *kampung* by a waterfall.
Buy fish with clear eyes.
Build something daily.

Flight –
Another country, another skin
to climb in. Didn't you know this place was a doorway
and you could travel for miles?

Scheherazade in the Care Home, Part I

& do you remember how all the king's horses bowed before him –

& do you remember cool sheets like muslin rain –

& do you remember running for the train in the night –

& do you remember the soldier's hand at your throat –

& do you remember holding yourself open, a little door
into the dark –

& do you remember when we came to this country we –

& do you remember how we made ambrosia salad
with mandarin pieces in syrup, Cool Whip, pecans,
tiny marshmallows soft and pink as a kitten's mouth –

& do you remember the sword hanging over my head –

& do you remember –

& when are we going home?

Scheherazade in the Care Home, Part II

"Yes, and the body holds memory"
– Claudia Rankine, *Citizen: An American Lyric*

Not too long ago you are in a room where she is just a
tiny slip of a thing in her zinnia print overcoat, already
faded, hiding small hands tucked into the knit blanket.
You bring her a silk scarf, peeled pomegranate, photos of
her grandchildren at birthday parties, 4th of July parades,
prom. *Oh*, she says, *there you are*, her smile bright and clean.
Her gaze a whole dark field. On the old TV set is a nature
documentary about how wolves change rivers, how fragile
equilibrium is, how we chase it like mouths in the dark.
Okay, Sharon, the nurse says not unkindly, and sets down a
cup of green jello.

Jade

You can tell the quality
of the stone by its clarity.

In that sense, they are little poems.
I carve them carefully, peashoot

earrings, thin pistachio foam
bracelet. Green like walking into

a clearing you didn't realise
was there, the sudden, bright gap,

sun marbling like mutton fat.
How precious the weight

in your hand, the weight
of your cool hand in mine.

Aubade with Court Ruling

Stand with me in the full fat American sunshine in all the places where we love each other: across state lines, courthouse steps, porch swings with seventeen fireflies for lamps, nothing forgotten or lost. Let me tell you about the orderly pursuit of happiness, summer undeterred, sucking stars on your shoulder, police vans swaying like sleep-warm bodies in the dark, the road always turning home. My beautiful boy, don't be afraid of loving. Are you getting all this down? There can be no question. There can be no doubt of liberty. Let me tell you who to love – no. Let me tell you how – yes: earth smelling of good mint, a skinny beanpole of a guy, the long lick of your back a furnace, sweet sweat pooling behind knees. The officer's expression like a door in the face and better a door than a fist, better a fist than your body bowing in the stand, good suit creasing, and better a body in a stand than in a tree. This is what I mean when I say unruly, you stubborn thing. Look at us, improper. Look at us, indecent. Look at us, incandescent and loving.

In June 1967, the Supreme Court of the United States unanimously ruled in Loving v. Virginia that interracial marriage was constitutional.

When My Daughter Asks I'll Say

November 9, 2016

Still here. We are still here
hanging up our washing,
buying milk, sorting glass
bottles from plastic,
paying taxes, watching
the evening news, hip propped
against the counter,
wondering if our mixed children
might pass as white today,
wondering if we can hold
our partner's hand today.
Let's get one thing straight
America, the sum
of the rest of our lives
will be spent
holding the line
we just crossed.
In a few hours
you'll stumble downstairs,
demanding pancakes and
pulpy orange juice.
For now, we crawl into bed.
I leave a little light on.
Remind me when
we wake, America,
we'll have to love each
other harder.

Nasty Woman Anthem

after Gwendolyn Brooks

won't you teach each other   about that wine stain   and club soda trick
how to walk cobblestones   in outrageous heels   how to choose
matte lipstick that lasts   won't you tell each other   to run for office
to start fires   stand up   take up space   be very difficult
& dangerous   when you least want to   when you're climbing
up the wall   it's open season for nasty women   and we go
through the greenwood, taking shots   in your hunting silence
                we are   beautiful   & sure   hand on heart
            it couldn't be helped   we wanted it so bad
these are instructions   for setting off bodies like dynamite
light us up and   stand well back   we sing sad   we laugh mad
we fight like hell   we kiss & tell   we drink Jack   we grab back.
In the same breath you take to say shrewd,   say shrew
say, some nerve you have,   and mean it as a damn compliment
there are so many uses for anger   and we know all of them
            take them out and polish them like good silver
we are sweet wildness   bright, fearsome things
            sun at our backs   and heady with all that life left to fight for

Marvin Thompson

Marvin Thompson has followed his family's tradition of migration (his parents were born in Kingston, Jamaica) by moving from London to mountainous South Wales. As a child, he was read Anansi stories and *1984*. Without these literary experiences, he may never have developed a love for narrative that led him to study an MA in Creative Writing. His poems and sequences have appeared in a number of magazines. These include *Poetry Wales, Wasafiri* and *Poetry Review*. Influences such as Howard Hodgkin, James Baldwin and John Coltrane attest to his interest in a wide range of art forms.

An Interview with Comedy Genius Olivier Welsh

1. When did you first know you wanted to be a stand-up comic?

'The sun has got his hat on. Hip. Hip. Hip,'
is what Gramps drawled during drives to sea air
where throats were eased from hayfever's gloved grip.
Those days kicked off by Gramps' Art Deco leer;
in shorts and Yankees cap he'd yawn or scowl
and switch from Dad's dub to Radio 3.
Then in old Jamaican patois he would howl:
'Watch the road. Stop trying to kill me!'

The taunting tone was a game for us three;
how long could we cork up our wild cackling?
I'd mimic Gramps till our Adam's apples jigged.
'You'll be a stand-up star,' Gramps said hoarsely.
I'd smell his grave's rain-wet soil whilst dreaming
of honouring him with wild Vegas gigs.

2. Was it difficult to turn your back on all the drugs?

Alone with coke after an O^2 gig
and with my lipstick wiped into a tearful smear,
I knelt on the loo floor, the walls red as figs.
Gramps' smoking jacket lay still as stale beer.

I drifted to Chestnut Farm's sweaty chores,
cows farting their methane into the air.
Sharon's eyes shone like Diana Dors'
and made our Year 10 work experience less austere,

clearing a path to summer's Dizzee songs,
uni, and that winter when we froze
in our first bedsit. That's where I let love wane,

my nights spent rehearsing jokes. 16 years on
her Facebook page lit that loo: *Pete proposed!*
How could I flush the stuff that numbed my pain?

3. What's the truth about how Tommy Mann was born?

2016 was a year of pain,
'Muslims go home!' spat from once-shy mouths.
Like Enoch Powell, Brexit turned tongues profane.
We were not so much divided by north and south
but by politicians' evil, post-truth views.
Have I Got News For You hosted my protest
of ironic racist quips in Gramp's royal blue,
a jacket Tommy wore with a puffed chest.

Tommy's first pub gig? I choked with fright.
His smoking jacket dripped with punters' spit
and his barbs about refugees' bums were booed.
So I studied, gave his voice more plum, more bite
and learnt his swagger: Tommy's path was lit.
To date on YouTube? Nine billion views.

4. What are your thoughts on comedians using the N-word?

There's a documentary with only nine views
that explains how the N-word spawned from a need
to dehumanise people of a dark hue
so cotton profits would feel less like greed

or sin. The word's history is not well known.
Its US uses are born from complex battles
but when it's packaged as an endearment I groan:
it still points to people owned as cattle.

With Pryor though, 'nigger' assumed beauty
which gave high fives to civil rights and shame.
Like joking about his own heart attack,

it gave him scope to poke fun brutally
at a land where folk sing Christ while crosses flame.
Compared to Pryor, all my jokes fall flat.

5. Which British comedians do you admire?

With Felix Dexter, even my jokes clap!
Yet he represents my heart's ambivalence.
From St Kitts to Slough – his gigs reeked of wet beer mats.
I'd watched his *Real McCoy* on VHS.
Mum's dusty tapes crackled with my first crush
and gave the air a Caribbeanness
that made me see Sharon's thick lips as lush.

But what happened to the rich, ragamuffin accents
and the sweet segregation of Auntie's airwaves
that gave voice to black stand-ups that nose dived?
Do Sky tell jokes about hair relaxants?
Where's the *Kumars'* equivalent on Dave?
I mimicked white males on TV and thrived!

6. But isn't it true that you've been influenced artistically by a host of white comedians?

By mimicking white men my career's thrived.
My Oxbridge Bernard Manning: what wild japes!
But to joke about John crows* and Brixton's Hive
that once served Sharon's patties and salted hake?

What's in the hearts of families that spoon
black bean sauce and beef on our high streets
then call the chefs Cs (and I don't mean 'coons'
which is Tommy's word for, 'Lives we should delete.')

I digress. It's true, Izzard wore slap and soared
with better gags and nails and cuter heels.
With me, who knows why the world is enthralled?

Tommy's tales are Corbett to the core.
Maybe then, the truth's just been revealed:
the black part of me's not funny at all.

In regions outside the Caribbean, John crows are known as turkey vultures and turkey buzzards.

7. Tell us about the controversy surrounding your hosting of the Oscars

Two years ago, I watched my bright skies fall
after ranting about Saint Obama's death.
Parliament announced they were appalled
while black activists denounced my very breath.
My management told me, 'Soften your quips,
or forget Vegas.' I gave in. Tommy raged
and turned to warpaint: rogued cheeks, rib-white lips.
In thigh-highs he stomped across each wild stage.

I found out six months late: Sharon had died.
I pleaded, 'Pull me from the Oscars job.'
In pain, I left my pen in Tommy's grip;
his wrath was a mask behind which I cried.
The Oscars aired – Tommy, in blackface, gobbed:
'The sun has got his hat on. Hip. Hip. Hip.'

Severn Sisters

After Patience Agbabi's 'Seven Sisters'

Dear Martina

After 19 years of lies, I guess it's time.
My little sis (your mum) was a dream girl.
Your dad? That Bristol Carnival weekend
I lured him into my house. You were a foetal child
listening to Coltrane's *Crescent*. He was a thin boy.
I got him drunk on gin and as noon grew dark

with rain, I locked him in my basement. *You're ape-dark*
was the kind of filth he'd text her come evening time
and she'd laugh it off: 'He's my strong, blue-eyed boy!'
That was the least of it. She'd sob like a weak girl,
scared he was cheating. 'You're so childish!'
I spat as one of our spa days came to an end.

She lifted her blouse, back pocked by butt ends.
It seemed simple: stuff your dad in the dark
for a few humid days. Let him cry like a lost child
in my basement. But that was a strange time,
London riots that last August. Girl,
was being tied up enough for a boy

who told me your mum's bruised ribs left him buoyed?
From his phone, I caused your mum pain that weekend
with messages supposedly for another girl.
My gut acid rose, each text sexually dark.
Your mum phoned me that Saturday teatime,
weeping. 'He's blanking me like a child.'

'You're carrying a shining tiara child,'
I sobbed. 'Don't lose it through stress.' *This boy
in my womb isn't yours.* It was the first time
she'd lied to him. Then came the end
when I called my sis *a tree-swinging darkie*
from his phone. We became nihilistic girls

for one, star-filled Saturday night. Loud girls
with nothing to lose. Because she was big with child,
I drank for two, your dad hogtied in the dark,
still unsure what I'd do with him. Boy oh boy
I gave him a good horse kicking at night's end,
birdsong stirring while I sang, 'Summertime...'

At the end, that thin boy blubbed, his face blood-dark,
his snot green as thyme. You were a fatherless child.
Sorry. And sorry if this girl doesn't press send.

The Thyme Traveller

Tucking me in that moonless night, mum sighed, 'Hello End Times
and hello World War III if Trump wins.' I was her cwtchy girl
and I believed her. I watched Hillary Clinton's end
on my phone. I was a detective's shy child
who knew that in a week the sky would be buoyed
by warheads carrying a hellish dark.

For five nights I prayed into the still dark,
surfing news sites a dead pastime.
On night six, a thought left me strangely buoyed.
Soon I'd be a memory of a girl
that no one held so I should, 'stop acting like a soft child
and visit London before the chance ends!'

(I often admonished myself at prayer's end).
I stood on tiptoes, Mum's lipstick dark
and kissed my tube-map poster. 'My wise, old child,'
Dad used to call me. Leaving home post-teatime
for a train to Paddington proved I was still that girl.
I walked out with Dad's card while he watched *The Lost Boys*

alone. Newport was full of snoring boys
when the whistle blew to signal my wait's end.
'Leicester Square's not ready for this grown-up girl!'
I thought as I pictured Wales' wintry dark
melting into a Camden ice-cream parlour where time
no longer ticked and the waiters danced like children.

The ticket lady called me an '*E.T.* child.'
Then she chuckled, 'We'll phone home.' My blood was a dead boy's.
At my table seat, I sobbed. Not for the End Times
or for the huge, lost lights of the West End.
I cried because, as the train hurtled through the thick dark,
my flimsy story marked me out as a girl

who wasn't wise at all. I was a fudge-brained girl.
Back home, my parents cwtched me up, their '*Indiana Jones* child.'
Yet, my favourite steak pie tasted sour and dark;
a sprig of thyme sat like a lonely boy
on its shortcrust top. What was the weirdest end?
I grew to hate the sight and taste of thyme –

it came to symbolise the lies adults feed children,
the boys and girls fooled, Dad's lying dark.
His rows with Mum were the real world's end.

The Earth Mother

Bryn:

The train slows: a scent sends me back to the lunchtime
on the school field when Dana was a plain Jane girl.
'Smell,' she said, baring the perfumed end
of her arm. I held her wrist like a scared child
and inhaled the wonder, my teenage heart buoyed
by our kiss, her lips Demerara dark.

I fought like a dog to resist the darkness
but would feel it filling my lungs come evening time.
Dana's throat trembled, 'He would've been our boy.'
'I bet you *did* smoke!' stopped her being my girl,
our flat silent as slate thrown by a child
into the Usk's enormous, muddy end.

Dana:

Desire made our lips meet in the end.
I'm sent back to that kiss by Coltrane's tenor dark,
his hot, wailing blues. I twirl like a child
abandoned to the amorphous time
the music keeps. Sorrow swirls in this girl
and nights conjure the shadows of my heartbreak boys.

At my potter's wheel I picture weather buoys
bobbing in the Atlantic and Leviathan's tongue end,
malt vinegar and the cod-loving girl
who cried and curled into her own darkness
on a tube train. Clay turns in my hands' time
to teapots and something dead as my child.

Bryn:

I digitise the voices of children
and twist them. I name the sculptures *Dead Boys*.
Years passed until that stalactite-still time
when I viewed Dana's *Tearoom* in Tate's turbine end.
Men with welted backs served tea – sweet and dark.
Patrons sipped and wept like boys and girls.

Dana:

Gut butterflies? I'll give them to the girl
who'd beg them back, who sensed a sad childhood
in Bryn's kiss before my heart's rose-dead dark.
She left him and he basked in his boyhood.
St Martin's marked her adolescence's end,
her dreams of bibs and clay distorting time.

Bryn/Dana:

I phone/he calls as I stroll like a feral child
through a field fragranced with day-end's dark,
time dissolving to scented girl/shy boy.

Misdemeanour

In that estuary dawn, loud flocks fled British time
and clouds hung as red as lipstick worn by naïve girls.
That wasn't where I'd want my pulse to end,
the breeze like the breath of a scowling child.
As the sniffers barked like gangland boys,
fear crawled through my chest to my throat's dark.

Sometimes there's a smell to dawn's near dark.
That day it smelt of the sea and summer's dead time.
Rain spat. I followed the dogs like a boy
who wants to become an ocean. Phil called women 'girls,'
he was old-school police, a 70s child.
In that marshland I asked myself, 'If this is Phil's end,

should I still hide his lies and will my love for him end?'
The wind rose. I knelt in the reeds by a mound of muddy darkness.
It was as if a body had been drawn by a child
who'd forgotten to add the limbs. 'It's not your time,'
they said then, 'Undercover? Ha! You're a black girl.'
In those reeds, Phil's face held the calm of a choirboy.

The truth is, he was a wide boy:
he told stories of a childhood with a drunk dad in Southend
to charm and manipulate his 'girls',
women who wouldn't rise rank by playing loose and dark
with the rules like he did. That was a different time –
but undercover and fathering a child?

Somehow they hushed it up. But that child?
I heard Phil boast about his sired boys.
I reported it and, green as garden-grown thyme,
met Phil in some cold café in Church End.
He ordered two Irish coffees. His kisses were dark
as liquorice and I became his top girl.

In the hospital I was the gobby girl
waiting to rid myself of his demon child,
its heart pumping and pumping in my womb's dark.
Post op, I cried and decided I'd bear a bounty of boys.
But I was anchored to Phil and that wouldn't end
so I moved out west, my memories consigned to time.

With officers gathered, Phil's lips shone like a child's.
How many boys and girls had he left in the dark?
Time slowed. I announced: 'He was a trooper till the end.'

The Tiger

My rifle shakes as my heart beats double-time
in this Helmand house lit by a singing street girl
whose soulful Pashto feels as close as my training's end
while my fellow soldiers are sat like children
hiding in the shadows – silent sweating boys
hoping this sniper can aim in the dark.

I am trying to slow my thoughts in this viscous dark
while Tomtom on GPS worries time
with his twitches and I signal to the boys
as the mark steps from a jeep like a proud girl.
I want control, I want to be that child
who slowed her pulse at the oche's sweet end.

I am aiming to cause a man's unnatural end:
my training hides in my chest's trembling dark.
Quivering fingers never took hold as a child:
between each pulse, my dart's release froze time,
my flexor muscles braver. The singing girl
has stopped, this room filling with the shouts of street boys.

I am sure Ted knows, no fooling that toff boy,
my chest tight as when 'Taff' spilled from his cake-end.
I let him sleep then cut his pubes – he laughed: 'You go, girl!'
I feel weighed down by his eyes and the darkness.
This mark's too real, my jitters distorting time.
How is it I had more steel as a child?

I am back there, the brittle cancer-ward child.
My thorax is filling with screams for my ex boyfriend.
I see his pic of my scarred chest. His tweet: 'It's go-time
for her fetish career!' His rugby career was ended
by my brothers. But they couldn't stop the dark.
My sobs in the bath. My breasts were a ghost girl's.

I am the link that will get us killed. Like a bitch-girl
the mark slaps one of his soldiers – I quake like a child.
He's at the door. A fly crawls my neck's dark:
the mark's some mother's boy some mother's boy
I am the White Death. The White Death has no end.
I am the White Death… the tattoo gun stalled time.

Now my white tiger prowls my breasts' dark.
This is for boys. Girls. Kids'. Christmas. Eid. Time.
The White Death. Pulse. Trigger. Pulse. *Has no end.*

Samantha

Luggage carouselled in Pacific standard time.
A black Barbie was dropped by a pouting girl.
I crouched down for it. The girl's grin was endless,
the same kind of smile I hoped for from Kai's children.
He felt more my man when he mentioned them, his jokes buoyed.
But then I pictured his granddad, Aid, in the dark

of a 1940s Kentucky noon where church hats were darkened
by woodland shadows. My gran watched time
pass through her camera's viewfinder, the crowd buoyed.
Her friends were all grinning pigtailed girls,
the rope just out of shot. Aid was still a child,
his burnt limbs blurred. That photo marked the start of the end

for my mum's lungs. She asked me, 'Please put this to an end.'
I froze, her bedside lamp pushing back the dark,
her yellow eyes turning me into a trembling child.
She pointed to her bag. Its leather was cracked like time,
the photo in a pocket made for girls
to zip secrets. 'They lynched him. He was just a boy.

Call me Mamma Bundren!' Her smirk was boyish.
Then tears trickled, the room's heat endless.
I gazed at the creased photo like a girl
infected by its terror and its darkness.
A date was scrawled: *12/7/41*. I heard time
grind. Mum's face looked faint as she lay childlike:

'This photo gave me nightmares throughout my childhood.
Your gran made me date a Ugandan boy
out of guilt!' Asleep, my mum's scent seemed beyond time
like my Tewkesbury gran whose words had soft endings
and a Kentucky twang that twirled round her darkroom,
a place that held more magic than Kodak girls.

In the airport's hotel room I dreamt Aid's white girlfriend
(a tall, sweet 16 who fled west with her child)
and my first Skype with Kai, my, 'Sorry,' sounding bitter and dark.
Us made my heart leap and leap like a boy.
In the shower, I prayed that our meeting wouldn't be the end.
In the cab, my neck pulsed in panicked time.

'My Nikon's my life,' I told Kai, the shore dark,
Kai's boy and girl chasing the sun's end.
We raced the children, smiling wide as time.

Leila

In the shadows of a Royal Gwent ward, God called time
on my DNR. My once sassy inner girl
sobbed with envy. Undressing at shift's end
I recalled how I'd act like a spoilt child
when my wife preened for work. I'd call her, 'Ladyboy!'
and let her grab my arms, our kisses rum dark.

Most afternoons I hide in the curtained dark
re-watching *The Wire* to kill time.
Like a toffee in the mouth of a doleful boy,
noise dissolves to 'Walk on By' sung by my girl.
When I found her, her bathwater was red as childbirth,
a Bloody Mary staining her life's end.

God's cruel game began in the West End.
The DKNY fitting room was dark
and I was there with black jeans – a child
mourning her dead Jamaican dad. A knock halted time.
I opened the door to a shy shop girl.
She asked to change the bulb, her cheeks boyish.

Her accent? Cape Town. Her freckles? Oh boy!
Her badge said *Sabrina*. That night in Crouch End
we laughed and sank shots. A week later, like schoolgirls,
we snuggled up and watched *Luther* in the dark.
Sunday nights were our enchanted ice-cream time.
I'd watch her sleep while scenes from my childhood

churned my gut. I knew I was being childish
but her Cape Town accent recalled school's skinhead boys
and PW Botha – his voice the vile sound of apartheid time.
When our first kiss came to its sweet, breathy end
hate invaded my lungs and made the world feel dark.
I tried to talk about it but I'm a reticent girl;

I clammed up and Sabrina became a good-time girl
who held each Bloody Mary like a newborn child.
'Is it my accent?' she'd ask in our bedroom's dark,
'No!' I'd snap and she'd run to one of her Tinder boys.
We decided to elope one June weekend,
our hearts cartoon bombs ticking, ticking time.

During anaesthetists' dark, empty time,
the sound of Sabrina's, 'Walk on By' hugs me like a child.
She's still my buoy, my girl, my wife, her voice endless.

Thanks and Acknowledgements

Thank you to Julia Bird and all at The Poetry School for their continued partnership on the *Primers* scheme, and all of the behind-the-scenes support that makes such a project possible.

Many thanks are also due to Jacob Sam-La Rose, selecting editor and mentor for *Primers: Volume Two,* whose insight, knowledge and generous advice was invaluable.

Finally, sincere thanks are due to everyone who submitted poetry for *Primers: Volume Two*, to the longlisted and shortlisted poets, as well as our three finalists.

Cynthia Miller:

'Yellow', after a poem by Ocean Vuong called 'On Earth We're Briefly Gorgeous' from *Night Sky With Exit Wounds* (Cape Poetry, 2017).

'How To Run Away', after a poem by Zeina Hashem Beck called "Naming Things", first published in *The Rialto* issue 84.

'Nasty Woman Anthem', after a poem by Gwendolyn Brooks called 'We Real Cool', from *The Bean Eaters,* (published by Harpers, 1960).

Marvin Thompson:

'Severn Sisters', after 'Seven Sisters', a poem sequence by Patience Agbabi, published in *Transformatrix* (Canongate Books, 2012).